DELAPRÉ A
NORTHAMPTON

A History
By Colin Spears

Publisher:
Desmondo Publications
17 Ringwood Close
Northampton NN2 8QG

ISBN
978-0-9553692-1-6

First Edition August 2006
Second Edition December 2012

British Library cataloguing in Publication Data.
A catalogue record for this book is available from the British Library.

Orders & Distribution:

Foda Ltd, The Stable Block
Delapré Abbey, London Road,
Northampton NN4 8AW
Tel: 01604 708675
E: friends@delapreabbey.org

Published by:
Desmondo Publications,
17 Ringwood Close,
Northampton NN2 8QG
Tel: 01604 844988
E: desmondo.publications@talktalk.net

Design and Print by:
Blayney Partnership Limited
Barn 3, Hall Farm, Sywell Aerodrome
Sywell, Northampton NN6 0BN
Tel: 01604 671714
www.blayneypartnership.co.uk

FOREWORD

This is the second edition of the Delapré Abbey History Book and publication has been enabled by a Grant from the Northamptonshire Community Foundation and Northampton Borough Council, for which Foda are extremely grateful. Sale monies are being allocated to the restoration of the third Victorian Greenhouse.

It updates aspects of the first edition and covers developments from 2006 - 2012, which led up to the Heritage Lottery Fund Bid in 2013 for £3.5m: If achieved, it will commence restoration of a very interesting nationally listed 'Grade 2 Star' building situated one mile south of Northampton Town Centre. (Satnav NN4 8AW). It is owned by Northampton Borough Council, who created the Delapré Abbey Preservation Trust in 2006. Both parties are keen to keep the Abbey in public use by utilising plans in the Bid, aimed at giving the public opportunities to support the Abbey in various ways and thus reduce it's annual maintenance costs.

It is also in the English Heritage area of the significant Battle of Northampton, which took place on 10 July 1460 during the War of the Roses. The exact location of the Battle site is being researched, with the object of preventing any local development on an English Heritage listed nationally significant Battle site.

The 'Abbey' with its immediate Parkland is regarded with great affection by the people of Northampton. They formed 'The Friends of Delapré Abbey'(Foda) which is an active Community organisation with its Office and a very pleasant Tea Room, in the Stable Block by the Abbey.

The author is a Life member of Foda and Blue Badge Tourist Guide, and since 1992 has conducted Tours and Talks about the Abbey and Gardens on site and around the County. This book has been written, so that its developing history can be shared with everyone who has an interest in the building and Northampton's local heritage.

Sadly over the Centuries much has been disposed of but earlier historians have provided a good background from the available evidence. I acknowledge here the work of Dr Joan Wake CBE, Mr W A Pantin, Rev R M Sergeantson: the assistance given to me by both the Northamptonshire Record Society and County Record Office; the County Library Records staff; Brian Stevens - the former Vicar of St Edmunds in Hardingstone; Officers of Northampton Borough Council; Councillors past and present; previous and current Chair Holders of the Preservation Trust & Friends of Delapré Abbey; Gary Dorrington; Tom Welsh; numerous local people; Rob Blayney and finally - the all important support of my dear wife.

Bibliography: Delapré Abbey Northampton - J. Wake & W.A Pantin 1959
Cover photos:
Front page: North West front of Delapré Abbey
Back page: The Inner Garden - July

CHAPTER SUMMARY

Chapter 1

CONVENT OF ST MARY DE LA PRÉ
C1145 - 1538

(St Mary of The Meadow)

One of the few remaining buildings in Northampton that can trace its heritage back to Norman times is a Country House converted from the former Convent of St Mary de la Pré (St Mary of the Meadow). The Convent and estate which were confiscated and dissolved by Henry VIII in 1538, are now known locally as - Delapré Abbey. It is situated on the south side of Northampton - leaving the town on the A508 South (M1) it is on the left hand side some 400yards after the cross roads by a Supermarket, if entering the town on the A508 from the A45 roundabout, it is on the right at the bottom of the hill. (Satnav NN4 8AW)

After the Norman conquest of England, King William 1st (1066 - 1087) created an Earldom for Simon de St Lis who, to establish and reinforce his new role in life, built Northampton Castle before 1100: the current Northampton Railway station was built from 1879 -1881 over the Castle remains. Earl Simon 1st also established the Cluniac Priory of St Andrew on the north western side of Northampton (the site location was probably in the area of the Semilong Working Man's Club in St Andrews road): it represented a branch of the reformed Benedictine Order that had been created in 910 at Cluny Abbey, Burgundy in France. He donated to the Priory several areas of land around the town; one of which was to the south of it near Hardingstone village. The Priory was ruled from Cluny Abbey.

The Cluniac order was supported by the Norman elite and Earl Simon 2nd, son of Earl Simon 1st, wanted to follow his father by creating a Convent of the same Order, close to the town. About 1145 he was no doubt in discussions with the Prior of St Andrews about his project and where the land might come from to support it, knowing of course exactly what his father had donated to the Priory on its establishment The Prior probably liaised with Cluny Abbey and obtained their agreement to release land in the Hardingstone area south of the town. He published his gift to the Earl in the form of a Charter (in the British Museum) granting the land for - a Monastery of St Mary where nuns may serve God and the aforesaid Virgin. The Convent became known as - St Mary de la Pre (St Mary of the Meadow).

Earl Simon 2nd endowed it with land in Hardingstone and elsewhere around the town; plus the churches of Earls Barton, Great Doddington and Fotheringhay; a Tun of wine at Pentecost (Whit Sunday) for celebration of the Mass and the right of collecting a daily cartload of wood from Yardley Chase.

No plans exist of what the Convent looked like but based on those elsewhere in England, the sketch on page 24, gives a maybe plan, as the development of the House fairly closely follows the layout of it. One of the first difficulties for the local Builder, as visitors can see, was the slope of the meadow down to the river Nene.

The Convent was therefore built about 1145 with local stone and timber around a courtyard, which contained the water well; probably under the supervision of the Prior of St Andrews. It would have had a Church, Cloisters, Chapter House, Dormitory, Refectory, Storerooms and a Visitors' facility. The Refectory was probably on the South side, which for some 8 months of the year received warm sunshine. Evidence exists that King Henry III gave grants of timber from local forests for repairs and rebuilding eg in 1232 ten beams for the repair of the Church and in 1258, five oaks for making the Refectory.

The existing House courtyard is probably the same size as that of the original Convent and it also has a covered well. There are three corridors - on the West, North and East side that were probably the original cloisters. At either end of the northern cloister, are two stone recesses for candles to throw light on the corners, as nuns went on their way to the nave for matins in the early morning.

On the eastern side of the Convent behind the Church Choir and surrounded by a wall, was the nuns graveyard. It is now part of the House inner garden with no evidence of its' earlier history; and a casualty of the transformation into a House, particularly by Zouch Tate in the early 1600's.

As the kitchen was probably on the south west corner, it is likely that the garden was just outside it and probably sloped uphill but it could have been landscaped level. This probably provided the herbs for the Convent. The land let to the local tenant farmers probably provided the vegetables and fruit needs, on the basis that a percentage came back as payment in kind. A small dairy perhaps located on the south west side of the Convent and probably run with local support, provided milk and butter.

Whilst the Prior of St Andrews reported directly to the Abbot at Cluny in France, unusually the Abbess at St Mary had the right of electing her successor subject to the approval of the Bishop of Lincoln who also paid occasional visits: these were notified by a horseman from the Bishops entourage in Lincoln, who brought a letter stating, for example, that the Bishop would be visiting in 2 weeks time…..causing the Abbess no doubt to liaise on such occasions with other Church leaders in the town…….but she probably burnt some midnight oil to ensure the administration was all in order for the visit…….One has to imagine here a small Convent immersed in the routine of Church life but also dealing with visitors who came in off the London road at the end of the drive, plus no doubt tenants who paid rent on their land properties - the Bishops visit was therefore a big event!!

The first Abbess circa 1145 was Azelina and then the record is blank until 1220 when Cecilia de Daventry was appointed; after her time the record is complete to 1538.(See Page 58 for the list) In all twenty Abbesses were recorded, seven of whom came from the following villages: - Cottesbrooke, Daventry, Moulton, Naseby, Sywell, Wollaston and Wootton. Two lists of nuns have survived over time and they are from 1530, which shows eleven nuns present in the Chapter House for the visit of the Bishop of Lincoln and December 1538, which gives the names of those nuns pensioned off after the closure of the Convent by Henry VIII as part of the general dissolution.

Records exist which show that all was not well in the Convent from time to time. In 1300 under Abbess Margery de Broke, three nuns named Ermentrude, Isabella and Matilda decided that the routine of the Convent was not for them and they ran off to live normally in the locality; where eventually they were discovered and excommunicated. Several years later Nun Agnes apparently appeared in the Choir dressed in a velvet gown and was also excommunicated; following this episode the Bishop of Lincoln persuaded and delegated the Vicar of Rothersthorpe to oversee the Convent. Despite his best efforts, Abbess Margery de Broke was excommunicated and resigned. Finally the Abbess of 1435 received a performance black mark from the Bishop, when he discovered on a visit that she had failed to keep up the admin paperwork - 'for the information of those that come after'.

The death of an Abbess would obviously have been a stressful time for the nuns and in 1333 there were major internal problems when a slim majority elected Isabella of Cottesbrooke. Arguments must have taken place and the general atmosphere would have been pretty grim.... The Bishop had to intervene and her rival - Catherine Knyvett, was appointed instead. Mealtime in the Refectory and prayers must have been strained for some time after that episode....Abbess Catherine Knyvett however succumbed to the Black Death in 1349.

From about 1145 - 1337 the nuns would have spoken French within the Convent but English when dealing with the visitors and tenants. In 1337 England, under Edward the 3rd, began the 100 years war with France and in 1362 the use of English was ordered for the Law Courts, as Norman - French was a dying language within the population. However the Speaker of the Westminster Parliament still uses Norman - French when he says ' La Reine le vau '(The Queen wishes it) when Bills become law after their third and final reading. Once a year at Pentecost (Whit Sunday) the Abbess and her nuns were obliged to have contact with the local townsfolk, because Earl Simon 2nd had decreed that they would receive the members of the Northampton Weavers Guild for blessing and prayers, and afterwards - partake of wine from the Tun given annually for the festival by the then Earl. A Tun is an old measurement and represents 252 gallons .....so 252 gallons x 8 pints divided by 365 days equals 5.5 pints (3 litres) per day through the year for Holy use and the balance perhaps for 'sippers' at Supper in the Refectory. Whoever had the key for access to the Tun was no doubt a popular nun.

There were three key events of a national nature which confronted the Abbess of the day: they were: 7 December 1290 - the arrival of Queen Eleanor's cortege, 10 July 1460 - the battle of Northampton during the War of the Roses and 16 December 1538 - the confiscation and dissolution of the Convent by King Henry VIII. Each is briefly described below.

Queen Eleanor's Cortege.

Queen Eleanor of Castile was the wife of King Edward 1st (1272 - 1307). Eleanor was the daughter of Ferdinand III, King of Castile and Leon. Their marriage in 1254, when she was aged 10 and he was 15, was primarily the consequence of scheming by his father - Henry 111, enabling Gascony to be part of the English King's heritage. The marriage was a good one by all accounts, their first child was born in 1257 and their 16th ......in 1284, the majority were girls. One child was born in Acre during a Crusade campaign and others in Bordeaux, Rouen and Caernavon - clearly a loyal, loving and well travelled Queen.

Eleanor died at Harby village, just west of Lincoln, Nottinghamshire on 28 November 1290. Her body was embalmed in Lincoln and a distraught King set out from there on December 4th with the cortege of his wife, heading for Westminster Abbey where it finally arrived on the 14th; the funeral took place on the 17th December. Overnight stops were made at Grantham, Stamford, Geddington (Northants), Northampton - the Convent of St Mary De la Pre, Stony Stratford, Woburn, Dunstable, St Albans, Waltham Abbey, West Cheap and Charing in London: a journey of some 150 miles on poor roads over 10 days in often unpleasant weather, at each location, the King had a Cross built in memory of his beloved Queen.

The afternoon of 7 December saw the Abbess of the Convent of St Mary De la Pre receiving the cortege of Queen Eleanor. Aware of the Queens popularity, the Abbess would have taken her coffin into the church where it would have been the subject of an all night vigil by the nuns; whilst King Edward probably stayed in Northampton Castle with other members of his loyal team. The next morning the cortege left the Convent pausing within sight of it, at the hilltop of the London road before the cross roads to Stony Stratford, so that on the instructions of the King and following an old Church custom for such a person, a piece of land on the left hand side could be consecrated for a future memorial to his late Queen and her stay in Northampton.

The magnificent Stone Cross memorial to Queen Eleanor was probably completed by 1293, but lost its Cross sometime in the period 1293 - 1460 because observers of the battle of Northampton in 1460, recorded that the Cross was missing. Over 712 years later, it still stands at the hilltop of the London road as a splendid example of medieval stonework and the love of a King for his Queen. The Stone Cross at Geddington is complete but of a different design and Waltham Cross is the only other remaining monument to Queen Eleanor, apart from her tomb in Westminster Abbey.

The Battle of Northampton 10 July 1460. (War of the Roses)

The Abbess would have been aware of the tensions within England caused by the families of York and Lancaster, as each wanted to have their son as successor to King Henry V1 (House of Lancaster); who had reigned since 1422. His Queen - Margaret of Anjou, was very determined to have their son - Edward Prince of Wales as the next King, but he was only 7 years old in 1460. The House of York were sure that they had the right of succession in the form of Edward Earl of March, who was born at Rouen on 28 April 1442. This war of succession was fought by the two families in England on and off from 1459 - 1487 and is now known as the War of the Roses - White for the Yorkists and Red for the Lancastrians.

In early July 1460, King Henry V1 held a Parliament in Coventry and had become aware that young Edward Earl of March, had travelled across from France with his Yorkist army plus the Earl of Warwick and was en route to the Midlands. Henry moved his army towards Northampton and on arrival at the Castle about 7th July, agreed with the Duke of Buckingham that a defensive position south of the river Nene should be used but not too close to the Convent. Queen Margaret of Anjou was left in the Castle.

The Abbess and her nuns were no doubt horrified at the thought of a battle literally on their doorstep but continued with their routine, conscious of the fact that their King was probably going to be in the battle himself. Meanwhile the Duke of Buckingham with the King's army of about three thousand men, were constructing ditches just south of the river Nene, with a steep side to the north, in a semi circular position over a front of about one mile, the design being to prevent mounted troops leaping over the position and overrunning trenches behind them towards the river. The Yorkists had gathered S/SW on the ridge (now the Ring road) which overlooked the Convent and the King's Army.

On 10 July the Abbess and her nuns were petrified to hear the sound of the Yorkist army of some three thousand men, as they charged downhill on the attack to the east of the Convent towards the Lancastrian position in front of the river Nene. The sound of hundreds of galloping horses and the battle cries of their riders carried by the wind over the meadow to the quiet of their Convent.

Due to the treachery of Lord Grey of Ruthin on the King's side, who let the Yorkists in through his defensive area, King Henry V1 was captured and a number of his key Earls / Dukes were killed; the battle having lasted just over half an hour. Henry was taken to the Convent overnight and then on to London as a prisoner the next day. The nuns cared for the wounded but the inevitable death of soldiers from gangrenous wounds caused a separate burial plot to be made for them to the east of the Convent which, following a sewer excavation in 1895, was discovered to be in the general area now covered by part of the south west corner of the Cottage garden. Henry's soldiers who could escape did so across the river Nene but many drowned, as it was swollen from the previous two days' rain. Queen Margaret left Northampton Castle and immediately headed North with the remaining Lancastrian forces, only to hear later that her son had been disinherited from the throne by Parliament in the Act of Settlement of 1460, which recognised the claim by Edward Duke of York formerly the Earl of March. She was, however, a formidable Queen and after three further battles was reunited with her King at the battle of St Albans in 1461, shortly after which Edward IV was proclaimed King; which is the national significance of the Northampton battle on 10 July 1460.

(Author's note). The Battlefield Trust (BFT) Internet (www.battlefieldstrust.com) of which he is a Member, maintain a keen interest in this Battle, as the actual location is the subject of dispute. The Trust held a meeting in July 2010 (550th Anniversary) at the Northampton Museum, and after some 4 hours of learned discussion and debate, the consensus was that there was no clear evidence of where the battle site is located - maybe just south of the River Nene and South east of Northampton or where the Golf Course is located, which is South of the Abbey. Hence their monitoring of any planned NBC development activity (proposals are in as at October 2012) which may well cause the loss of vital evidence, particularly in the area of and surrounding the Golf Course. English Heritage has an ongoing interest in the preservation of the battlefield. The BFT local active Member is: Mike Ingram - Mobile 07738 908808)

The Dissolution of the Convent in 1538.

Henry VIII is well known in English history for his six wives and what happened to them…..four died but two were beheaded in the Tower of London to make way for his next Queen……What is perhaps not so well known is that he is responsible for the loss to future English generations of their rich cultural history going back to Saxon times; due to his greedy pursuit of money to fund his establishment of the English Church. He achieved this through Parliament by confiscating and selling off all valuables and the majority of buildings, from virtually all of the Abbeys, Monasteries, Nunneries and related organisations throughout England from 1536 - 1547 when he died.

The cause of his behaviour was his inability to obtain from the Pope a dispensation to set aside his 22 year old marriage to his first wife - Catherine of Aragon, who was unable to give him a male heir: he eventually married Ann Boleyn secretly in 1533 but she died on the scaffold in 1536. They had a daughter - Elizabeth (later Elizabeth 1st).

Thus it was that in 1536 the Convent was visited by the King's Commissioner, who demanded money and property from the Abbess. She gave him the sum of £266, an enormous sum of money in those days, plus grants of land and the rent arising from them, in the firm belief that the matter was now closed. However on 16th of December 1538 the Kings Commissioner reappeared and in a meeting in the Chapter House, the Abbess who had been in her post for over 30 years, was told - that the Convent must be surrendered to the King and he had the appropriate document with him (in British Museum). She would receive a good Pension in view of her age and service and the remaining nuns would receive a nominal Pension too, but they were no longer able to remain there. So probably before Christmas 1538, the Abbess and her nuns retired to the town to get over the shock of losing their Convent way of life, with the nuns beginning to realise that they would have to adjust and establish themselves into the new society that Henry was creating by his actions against the Catholic Church.

Records of the nuns' routine and the Convents financial administration of its lands are sadly not available. The Commissioners Report of December 1538 shows that it had land in 18 parishes of Northampton, 3 in Buckinghamshire, and 3 in Leicestershire in addition to endowed land (from Earl Simon 2nd) in Hardingstone and Far Cotton. All these lands and the Convent now belonged to King Henry, and his administrators would ensure that they received the best price in disposing of them. It is on record that the Commissioners removed from the Convent two Chalices and a Pyx (a small Communion box), which were taken to London.

So as the new year of 1539 dawned, the Convent was being emptied of it's contents and in London the team of ruthless administrators led by Thomas Cromwell (Secretary of State and Master of the Rolls), noted the effects as they had done for countless other Holy places in England. Their role was to sell the confiscated land and treasures to finance the King's establishment of the Church of England. The administrators removed lead from the Convent roof to the value of £136 and also sold off the three Convent bells. In 1539 the land was let to a tenant and in 1543, the administrators agreed a deal with John Mersh from London for the property. He sold it in 1546 to Sir John Tate a former Lord Mayor of London and businessman thus creating the Tate family's link to Delapré.

Chapter 2

THE TATE FAMILY
1546 - 1764

Sir John Tate former Lord Mayor of London and City businessman purchased Delapré circa 1546, from a London property speculator named John Mershe. It was for his son Bartholomew, who was married to Anne Saunders of Harrington near Kettering and his grandson also named Bartholomew from their marriage. As the site was semi derelict after some 7 years of neglect, it is doubtful if the family actually moved into Delapré but they probably had an appropriate House in the area. Anne however did not care for the life her husband led, always on the Continent and when at home, drinking with friends of King Henry V111: so she divorced him and remarried Sir Thomas Longueville of Little Billing and Wolverton but that marriage did not last either and she remarried for the third time - Andrew Wadham. In 1548 Anne took up residence in Delapré with third husband Andrew and her son - Bartholomew Tate from her first marriage, in whose name the property was registered.

By 1548 most of the land from the original Convent had been sold off for Henry V111 by Thomas Cromwell, his ruthless Administrator; who pursued and processed the sale of dissolution properties throughout England, which resulted in the greatest redistribution of land, and property the country has ever seen. The boundaries of the Delapré estate sold off to the Tate's were to the North - to the river Nene, to the East probably to the parish boundary of Great Houghton, to the South the parish boundary of Hardingstone and to the West the natural boundary of the London road.

One has to imagine the state that the Convent was in some 10 years after King Henry V111 had confiscated it. Parts of the stone and timber building may have been taken by local people for 'recycling' purposes but to all intents and purposes it was derelict; with rotting timbers over and around the Church and roof supports for the building, as some parts were nearly 400 years old. The opinion of Anne and husband Andrew as they rode up the lane to the Convent from the London road, has to be speculation, as are the comments of son Bartholomew, who may well have been told by his father - Bartholomew Tate, that he would inherit land and property in Northampton............ However they got on with the task of converting the Convent into a House no doubt with labour from the town; assisted by the fact that they probably had lodgings there whilst the work was being carried out.

Assuming that the Church had no roof, the initial build would have been to cover it and create accommodation for House staff on the first floor, sub dividing up the former Nave into small rooms which can be seen today. Two Tudor style doorways were built into the former Nave wall on the North cloister side, one of which led up into a Newel (Nual in Norman French) staircase; which was built from the Cloister to the new first floor. This style of staircase around a central column was quite common in Norman and medieval buildings because it was designed for a sword to be used in the right hand defending the upper floor - memories were no doubt still around from the War of the Roses and the battle of Northampton some 90 years earlier....... (see photo 4 on page 24).

This work was probably carried out by Anne's son Bartholomew Tate who, on marriage, no doubt adapted other rooms of the former Convent for reasonable family use within the household budget. He died about 1572 and was succeeded by his son William, who was knighted by King James 1st in 1606 and appointed as a local Justice of the Peace and MP for Northamptonshire in 1614, he died in 1617. William, given his social standing in the area would have continued to improve the House accommodation at Delapré but it was his son - Zouch, born in 1606, who initiated major conversion.

Zouch Tate having grown up in the surroundings of a then partially converted Convent, must have had some clear views on what he would do to improve the accommodation if he had the opportunity which he eventually got. Before his death in 1651 he rebuilt: -the West front (facing the visitor on arrival) with two splendid curvilinear gables, one of which remains; the entrance and castellated wall behind it; the entire East side incorporating a big kitchen and behind that some outbuildings for a dairy and laundry. In order to build the outhouses he knocked down the remainder of the Church Altar and destroyed the vault which contained amongst others the coffin of Earl Simon 2nd, the founder of the Convent in 1145. It seems that he did not rebuild the South front, he either died before his plans could be realised or his finances expired or it was considered suitable for the time being.

Zouch Tate was clearly a person who had a local reputation for initiative and getting on and doing things because in 1640 the Mayor of Northampton and his Councillors took their Carriages out to Delapré to inform him that they had elected him as MP for the town - he had no prior knowledge of their intent...!! Zouch lived in interesting times, Charles 1st had ascended to the throne in 1625 and then upset everyone by marrying Henrietta Marie, a French Catholic. He did little to dispense the common belief that he had become one too and thus began a constitutional battle with Parliament, which he ignored and directly ruled the country from 1629 - 40. Zouch was therefore elected MP in the Parliament which saw the constitutional clash between it and the King gradually build up and result in the civil war of England from 1642 - 46; he saw the rise of Oliver Cromwell during the war and the eventual execution of Charles 1st on 30 January 1649 in Whitehall.

Zouch Tate died in 1651 having achieved his boyhood dream of creating from the no doubt poor buildings he remembered in his youth, a family House which apart from the south front rebuilt nearly 100 years later, still stands today. William was the son of Zouch Tate and as the family coffers were probably fairly empty after his father's building programme, he made no changes to the House. He was however appointed

High Sheriff of the County in 1670. Bartholomew was William's son and it would seem he too contributed nothing to the House, content no doubt to rest on his grandfather's memory. He died in 1704 and his son - also a Bartholomew - eventually married Arundel Stratford of Overstone and it was their daughter - Mary Tate - who married Charles Hardy, a naval officer in 1749.

Charles Hardy received Delapré Abbey as a Wedding present from his in laws! Bartholomew and Arundel Tate no doubt thinking that he would have the money to update, maintain and develop the House in the manner that their daughter Mary was accustomed...as some parts of it were decidedly 'tired' and little had been done in the 100 years since Zouch Tate died.

Once again in Tate history childhood memories resulted in the House development. Mary foresaw the need to have a decent formal Dining Room and Withdrawing Room for their guests and on the first floor above it, accommodation for the family and their visitors. This would replace the by now inadequate arrangements in the South Wing which probably had not been modified by Zouch Tate in the 1640's. Sadly after just under two years of marriage, Mary died in 1750 but Charles Hardy followed his beloved wife's wishes and rebuilt the South Wing probably between 1751 - 54; it stands today and is very impressive. His in laws may have lived to see the new build but they had died by late 1755.

Charles Hardy's Naval career developed, he became a Rear Admiral and received a Knighthood from King George 2nd on his appointment as Governor of New York, where he was in post from 1755 - 1757. As a consequence of his career, he spent little time at Delapré but when he did, he was conscious of the need for decent stables and horse accommodation. Thus prior to his appointment in New York, he built circa 1753/54 the attractive Coach house and Stable Block. Whilst Governor of New York he obviously reflected on his future life and career and he decided to advertise Delapré to be let in the Northampton Mercury edition of March 18th of 1756. Records are incomplete but in 1762 it was let to two surgeons - Lyon and Litchfield, who used it for their patients during inoculations.

In early 1764 Charles Hardy eventually sold the House to the Bouverie family for the sum of £22,000 after he had been elected MP for Rochester. The person who provided the money was probably Mary Clarke, the mother of Mary Bouverie (nee Clarke) for her grandson.

Chapter 3

THE BOUVERIES
1764 - 1946

Research by local Historian Gary Dorrington has clarified the intricate web of the Bouverie family and it is now much clearer who probably provided the money to buy Delapré Abbey from the Tate's. The new owner in 1764 of Delapré was Edward Bouverie, the second son of Sir Jacob Bouverie (created Baron of Longford and Viscount Folkstone in June 1747) and his wife Mary (nee Clarke) whose family lived in Hardingstone - she died on 24 November 1739. It is considered that it was her Mother - Mary Clarke who, following the death of her husband in October 1740, had the money and local knowledge to purchase Delapré Abbey in the name of her grandson Edward in 1764.

It was a timely event, as in June 1764 Edward married Harriet Fawkener. She was probably the society lady of London at the time and was so attractive, that Sir Joshua Reynolds painted a portrait of her. Edward's eldest brother was created Earl of Radnor in 1765 and presumably already had property appropriate to the appointment.

The Clarke local association is that Bartholomew Clarke was the second son of a farmer from Hardingstone, who went on to become a noted Wine Cooper and Merchant of the City of London; he died on 17 October 1740 aged 68 and a Memorial plaque to him and his wife Mary, who died 19 March 1768, is by the altar in Hardingstone Church. Their only daughter - Mary Clarke, married Jacob Bouverie and thus through the second son Edward, began the Bouverie relationship with Delapré.

The history of the Bouverie family shows that in 1568 Laurence des Bouveries, a 27 year old Fleming (now part of Belgium), settled in Canterbury with his wife Barbara van den Hove. One of their descendents was a Jacob Bouverie who married Mary Clarke from Hardingstone.

Over the years as a Blue Badge Guide, the author has often been asked whether the Bouverie family name is related to the late Jackie Kennedy's maiden name and family in America - she was the widow of President John Kennedy who was assassinated in 1963. If only.........her family origins however were in the village of Pont St Esprit, Arles in southern France, where a Michel Bouvier circa 1815, set out for the USA and established himself in Philadelphia.

Edward became MP for Northampton in 1780 and he is the person who added 'Abbey' to Delapré, to reflect its Convent history. As MP he held the post for 20 years, during which time he saw William Pitt as Prime Minister and experienced the parliamentary atmosphere of the America colonies war for independence, problems in Ireland with regard to the disposal of revenue monies and the reaction to the French Revolution: he died in 1810 and was succeeded by his eldest son Edward b1767, there were two other sons and five daughters from the marriage.

Edward who took over the estate in 1810 on the death of his father, had married on 10 March 1788, Catherine the only daughter of William Castle. Their marriage produced four sons - Everard William was the eldest followed by Charles who died without being married; Francis Kenelm born in 1798 more of whom later and James the youngest son, who also died without being married.

As he settled into life at Delapré, Edward occupied himself in politics and as a Liberal, he was a staunch supporter of the Reform Act which was passed in 1832 when he was 65 years old; he retired from Parliament shortly afterwards. The effect of this Bill was to give voting power to all householders in the country paying an annual rent of £10 and upwards and political power to manufacturers, merchants and shopkeepers. Wealthy Peers and other capitalists could no longer ' buy' seats in Parliament and thus over time Parliament was transformed as Members became responsible to their electors.

Whilst Edward was enjoying his Parliamentary life, he realised that knowledge and information were becoming an important factor in the social circles he moved in and for his family; the British empire and British industry were expanding and the invention of steam had the potential to create railway lines across the country supporting towns and industry. He therefore decided that Delapré Abbey needed a Library…and after no doubt much thought and discussion, it was decided to demolish the Southwest wing with its attractive gable front and rebuild it to blend into the South wing, built some 70 plus years previously by Admiral Tate.

Thus in the period between 1820 - 1840, the south west wing was demolished and a new Gothic style wing was built providing a spacious library on the ground floor and improved Bedroom accommodation on the first floor. As visitors view it today….and it is a matter of architectural taste and opinion….it really does look like a 'conversion that should not have happened'. Apart from the Library, maintenance was no doubt carried out regularly to the Abbey because his family lived there.

The 1851 Census shows that in residence were Edward and Catherine, 3 unmarried daughters and two daughters in law - they were supported by 12 Maids, 2 Butlers, 2 Footmen, 2 Grooms and a Gardner; the Estate figures were - 1 x Farm Bailiff, 6 Labourers and a boy in the Garden, 33 men and 6 boys on the Farm, 1 Mason and his labourer, 2 Carpenters and 2 Sawyers. No doubt the income from the estate ensured that all concerned has a reasonable living standard. Edward died in 1858 at the age of 91, no doubt quite content that his Library had been built and the papers and books it contained were full of the new Victorian age developments.

Everard William Bouverie was 69 when he took over the estate following his father's death. He had married Charlotte on 3 March 1816, she was the daughter of Colonel

Hugh O'Donel from Newport Pratt in Mayo Ireland. Sadly there were no children from their marriage but he had made a very creditable military career earlier in his life, in which he rose to the rank of General - he fought in the Iberian Peninsula war in Spain, was ADC (Aide de Camp) to the Duke of Wellington at the battle of Waterloo (18 June 1815 - there were over 15000 British dead but Napoleon's French Army lost the battle with over 30000 dead and he was later exiled to St Helena) and finally Everard had been made Equerry to Queen Victoria.

Prior to taking over Delapré, Everard and his wife probably lived in the Abbey but maintained a keen interest in local matters, as records indicate that he endowed schools in Hardingstone and Far Cotton after retirement from military life, their location however is not known but research on Mary Bouverie (died 1943), indicates that in Far Cotton it was probably the 'Old National School'. During Everard's tenure at Delapré he no doubt maintained the property as required, but probably in 1859 (the year after his father's death) he replaced the circular stairway from the ground to the upper floor with a more modern style that can be seen today. This apparently is because he disliked the creaking sounds from it when no one was around, which rumour said was either the ghost of LadyRosslyn, the eldest daughter of the first Edward Bouverie, or the ghosts of Nuns past who were fascinated by the view from the first floor.......

He updated the rental agreements for the estate which, in view of later developments, had probably not had the attention and administration under his ageing father that they deserved. Everard was however conscious of the fact that there was no heir to the Abbey. At some time in the early 1860's he became aware that someone claiming to be the son of his late brother Francis Kenelm Bouverie, who had died in Ireland in 1837, was, as his nephew, making a claim to the estate..........A court case followed in which the identity and family relationship were clearly established and thus on the death of Everard in 1871, his nephew John Augustus Sheil Bouverie (John A S) took over Delapré Abbey and estate - but who was he and what are the family connections?

John A S was the son of Francis Kenelm Bouverie, the third son of the marriage from Edward & Catherine who took over Delapré in 1810. Francis had lived as a boy at Delapré but then joined the Army, where he was commissioned and served as a Lieutenant with a Regiment based in County Derry, Ireland. In 1826 he married at the age of 29, a Miss Sheil of Derry Castle, Dawson, County Derry who was 19 years of age and apparently a very attractive young lady. James Bouverie, his brother, travelled over from Delapré to be at the wedding no doubt to report back to their father the details of it...........

After promotion to Captain, Francis decided to sell his Commission and settle down in Derry Castle with his wife and the monies from the sale of it plus an annual allowance of £100 from his father Edward in Delapré. In 1836 a son was born and interestingly given the name of John Augustus Sheil, the latter being the mother's maiden name. Francis Kenelm Bouverie died in 1837 and the £100 annuity he received from his father in Delapré ceased, leaving his widow to cope with life and a very young son.

On the death of his father, John A S was looked after by his mother, who married twice after the death of her first husband Francis. At about the age of 12 years he was sent to School in Carrickfergus near Belfast and on leaving, sought employment that provided accommodation and a regular income. He therefore joined the Irish Constabulary and then enlisted in the 4th Dragoon Guards (a Cavalry Regiment) as a Private soldier. He did well in the Army and was promoted to the rank of Corporal with the job of being Orderly to Sir Henry Smith, one of the Regiment's senior officers. During this period it seems that he was unaware of his Bouverie family background and Delapré Abbey.

In 1860, at the age of 25 years, John A S married Jane aged 33 and they lived at Derry Castle in Ireland. Their first child was born in 1861 and named Francis Kenelm after John's father, followed by Caroline in 1863 and Mary in 1865. John Augustus Sheil named after his father, was born in 1867 in Staffordshire, as was his younger sister Catherine in 1871, the youngest of the family was Gertrude who was born at Delapré in 1875.

After his marriage, John A S became aware of his family background perhaps through his mother if she was still alive but more probably through his relationship as Orderly to Sir Henry Smith, who, as a senior Army officer, would have known about General Everard Bouverie and might even have met him. Consequently in the early 1860's John A S petitioned the recently created Court of Probate and Divorce in London, to formally establish his relationship as the son of Francis Kenelm Bouverie and thus grandson to Edward and nephew to Everard. His petition was accepted and it seems likely that after this event the family moved to England about 1866, to the village of Brewood, west of Cannock in Staffordshire, because the 1881 census shows it as the birthplace of two children - John A S - 14 years old in 1881 and Catherine who was 9 years old.

Thus in 1871 on the death of Everard, his nephew - John A S Bouverie at the age of 34 became the heir to Delapré Abbey and moved in, unaware that his family were to be the last of their name to own the estate. John was elected Member of Parliament for Northampton and in view of his duties with such a role, he decided to improve parts of the Abbey which had been neglected over the preceding years. On the south east side he built a large Conservatory (demolished in 1958) and Billiard Room but it was the Tate South Wing from the early 1750's with it's Dining Room, Withdrawing Room and Saloon - the area between the Library and Withdrawing Room, that were the prime target of his improvements. Best quality wallpaper was used together with attractively carved wood coving and in the Dining Room and Withdrawing Room (Borough Museum store facilities at present), beautifully decorated ceilings featuring cameo family members and birds from the recently discovered lands of Africa and Australia, were all set off by large mirrors above the attractive marble fireplaces (see page 26 - 27). As part of the South wing, both rooms had a very pleasant view across the lawn towards Hardingstone. Plate glass windows also replaced the Tate originals from the 1750's and a limestone balustrade was erected on the roof of the South front, similar to that on the roof of Castle Ashby House. John A S placed his monogram in the ceiling of the Saloon where it can be seen today (see photo 6 on page 25).

All of these improvements required money and with his duties as MP, it is very probable that the estate and rents etc which had not had the financial attention needed for some 50 + years, fell even further behind in providing an income which matched the Abbey expenditure. One funding opportunity was seized by John A S, when he was approached by Silvanus Wreford who founded the well known Wrefords Transport Company in Northampton. He had recently moved up from Devon and was keen to take up the tenancy to Home Farm on the east of the estate. The Wreford family had the tenancy for many years and gave it up in the early 1950's.

Despite the financial pressures created perhaps by his view on what his living standards should be, given his local and Parliamentary role; John A S, probably conscious of his family history and responsibilities over the years, decided that a family vault should be built in Hardingstone churchyard. Sadly in the Spring of 1891 he and his wife Jane learnt that their eldest son Francis Kenelm, who had emigrated from Ireland to Canada, had died at Lacolle in Quebec Province; his body was embalmed, transported back to England and became the first family member to be laid to rest in the family vault on 12 May 1891.

A further disaster was to strike the Abbey on 24 June 1893, when a severe fire caused the East Wing to burn down, this was the Wing with the Kitchen in the north east corner that Zouch Tate had built in the 1630's. John A S by this time was in poor health and no doubt his son with the same name became responsible for the administration of a rebuild from the insurance - it is however possible that the insurance monies did not cover the costs and family capital was used to supplement them.

Thus when John A S died on the 8th December 1894 aged 58 to be buried with his eldest son in Hardingstone; his second son, the younger John A S, inherited Delapré at the age of 27 years and confirmed what he had probably discovered one year previously - that the estate was not in good financial shape. Regular building maintenance on the Abbey had been neglected and those parts built some 150 - 250 years by the Tate family, needed a lot of money to restore them and it was not available from the family account.

It is likely that John A S had poor health and he probably could not see himself taking up a job which would enable him to borrow money and repay it at either the regular payments needed or over the loan period required. His sister Mary was still single at 30 years of age and all her sisters had married - work for her in 1895 at the income level needed, was definitely not possible in those far off days...... His mother was still alive but she was an elderly 64 years and no money was available from her family... So the options were - He could sell the property...but he discounted that on family history grounds, estate land could be sold to start a renovation plan...but that was also discounted perhaps because the money it would raise would be far short of the capital needed.... or they could perhaps let the Abbey and see what happened.....The younger John Augustus Sheil Bouverie was still single and made the decision to let the property in 1896 to John Cooper and his large family, who was a Boot and Shoe manufacturer from Northampton.

Thus in 1896 the younger John A S and his sister Mary moved with their mother Jane, into Hardingstone House in the village of the same name. They no doubt all reflected on the tragic early death of Francis Kenelm in Lacolle, Quebec, Canada who would have inherited the Abbey but life continued to take it's sad toll on the family - Jane was buried in the family vault on 22 October 1903 aged 72, tragically followed by her second son John A S on 6 May 1905 at the young age of 38. Mary Helen Bouverie at the age of 40 years thus inherited the responsibility of Delapré Abbey from the day of her brother's death.

Mary Bouverie continued to live in Hardingstone House after the death of her brother in 1905 but the following year on 3 September 1906 came the news that John Cooper, the Delapré tenant, had died; his family gradually moved out of the Abbey, which then stood empty for several years. Mary decided to remain at Hardingstone House rather than have the emptiness and memories of Delapré. By 1914 prior to the commencement of World War 1, she felt able to return to her family home having no doubt received professional support on estate land and financial management, enabling her to fund maintenance for the House and thus feeling more secure in it. On 28 March of that year, to the excitement of many local people, a Bleriot plane landed in Delapré Park and a Northampton Independent photographer used his initiative to go up in it and claim 'the first passenger flight from Northampton' and photographed the town from the rather rickety rear seat !!

Mary occupied herself with an interest in farming matters on the estate and developed an interest in the law. She became a Justice of the Peace and Magistrate in 1926 and later Chair of the newly formed Juvenile Panel for Northamptonshire. Hardingstone connections enabled her to maintain a keen interest in Sunday school activities there for over 20 years and she was the benefactor for the playing field in the village - Bouverie Road is named after her family. She had a keen interest in welfare and became the only female member of the Northampton Hospital Board before being elected its President in 1938. In view of her work at Northampton Hospital, she became a Governor of St Andrews Hospital too. An active member of the Women's Institute, Mary later became Chair of the County Federation. The RoadMender Club movement interested her and she gave the old National School in Far Cotton to the Movement as a Club, this was probably the School that Everard Bouverie had endowed in the 1850's when the National School movement became active.

On the farming side she won many awards with her Jersey cattle and in 1937 began to breed the rare Red Poll cattle which, with her famous large white pigs, maintained the Trophy count from key agricultural shows around the Midlands. She relaxed from her administrative and farming roles by playing golf to County standard.

In 1937 she was awarded the OBE for her services as a JP and to Northampton Hospital. In 1938 the estate advisors caused her to sell off a large part of it but about 1000 acres of land was still left in Hardingstone, Great Houghton, Weston Favell and Boothville. In 1938 at the age of 63 years, she was beginning to suffer from rheumatoid arthritis and with the start of the Second World War in September 1939, she must have wondered what next for Delapré Abbey and the estate.

In September 1940 the War Office requisitioned Delapré Abbey and it's immediate surrounding lands for military purposes. Mary Bouverie initially stayed in the Stable Block but then moved out to Pond House in Duston in early 1942. Her health was deteriorating and in November 1942 with the assistance of her bailiff Mr Ansell, she returned to the Delapré Stable Block where she died on Wednesday 20 January 1943 aged 77 years. She was cremated and buried in the family vault at Hardingstone church four days later on 24 January.

The heir to the property was Mary Bouverie's nephew, Major Uthwatt Bouverie, the son of her sister Catherine. After the end of the Second World War in 1945, the property was still under War Office requisition but following negotiations with Northampton Corporation, he decided in 1946 to sell the Abbey and 586 acres of estate for the sum of £56421 (2012 value is £1,914,930), thus ending the Bouverie family association with Delapré after 182 years.

In closing this chapter, it must be recorded that the Bouverie family motto from their Coat of Arms, which is displayed in stained glass on the large window as you ascend the main stairs rebuilt by Everard Bouverie in 1859, is 'My Country is dear to me but freedom is more precious'. (See inside front cover).

MAYBE PLAN - ST MARY DE LA PRE (c1145 – 1538)

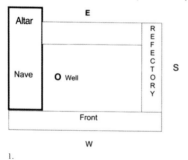

1.

2.

3.

4.

1. Maybe Plan of the Convent (see page 8)

2. Memorial Plaque - Dame Joan Wake CBE
   (see page 38)

3. NW Cloister Candle Recess (see page 8)

4. North Cloister Tudor Door
   & Newel Staircase (see page 15)

5.

6.

7.

5. Bouverie Library (see page 18)

6. John Sheil Bouverie Coat of Arms
   on Saloon Ceiling (see page 21)

7. WW2 B Platoon Door
   1940 -48 (see page 32)

8.

9.

8. Dining Room Ceiling Boar Feature
9. Dining Room Ceiling Coving
10. Dining Room Fireplace

10.

11.

12.

13.

11. Withdrawing Room Coving

12. Withdrawing Room Clock Feature

13. Withdrawing Room Ceiling

14. Withdrawing Room Fireplace & dust protected storage items

14.

Chapter 4

THE PARISH CHURCH FOR DELAPRÉ
ST EDMUNDS AT HARDINGSTONE

The village of Hardingstone is on a ridge to the south of Delapré Abbey and can be reached by leaving the Abbey and turning left onto the A508 and then following the sign posts at the A45 roundabout. The Church is on the right hand side of the road in the village.

Following the establishment of the Church of England by King Henry VIII, it was natural that both the Tate and Bouverie families chose to support the local parish Church of St Edmund in Hardingstone. The Church can trace its history back to at least 1223 when the first Vicar is recorded and it is named after Edmund the East Anglian King, who died from arrow wounds at Hoxne in Norfolk on 20 November 869 defending his Kingdom from the Danish invaders. In 903 his body was recovered and is interred at Bury St Edmunds.

The Church with its small tower is built with Northampton ironstone giving lovely soft colours in any season and blending well with the green grass and trees in the graveyard. The Rev Beverley Hollins has taken over from Rev Brian Stevens, who retired in 2012. He was responsible for initiating the extensive repair work costing over £250k with the assistance of English Heritage, the Church was actually shut from July 1992 to 24 December 1994 to enable the majority of the work to be done. The result is visually very pleasing to the visitor, who may wish to visit the Tate and in particular, the Bouverie families' heritage.

The Tate family would have used the Church and there is evidence in the Tower of work funded by Zouch Tate circa 1630-40; he effectively designed and built the West, North and East fronts of the Abbey that we see today. Sadly there is no other definitive association with the Tate family. The Bouveries, however, made it their family Church and on the walls either side of the Altar, are memorial plaques to generations of the family - superimposed on the south wall by a diamond shaped family crest. In the Tower base on the south wall is a large, decorative, wooden board with details of village charities supported by General Sir Everard Bouverie and other notable local persons. From 1868-1870, he funded a major restoration of the Church and the congregation showed its appreciation by placing a stained glass window behind the Altar.

In 1941 the congregation was concerned that the Bouverie Memorial Window could be destroyed by war damage from bombs etc and it was therefore removed to a safe place - so safe - that no one could remember where it was located when the time came to reinstall it!! Brian Stevens, the retired Vicar, suspected it is in the Bouverie Vault but...that is bricked up ....so the mystery remains!!

On the left hand side of the Altar is a large sculpture to Bartholomew Clarke and his wife Mary who died in 1768. There is reference to him being the father of 'Lady Bouverie' and this would be Mary Clarke, his daughter, who was the wife of Sir Jacob Bouverie, it was their son Edward who received Delapré as a gift in his name, from his mother in 1764.

The Bouverie Vault is unmarked but lies some 25 yards up on the right hand side of the entrance path to the Church; a 6-inch high metal chain fence in the shape of a square surrounds it. It contains Francis Kenelm Bouverie who died in Canada aged 38 and was buried on 12 May 1891, John Augustus Sheil Bouverie (father of Francis) who died aged 58 on 8 December 1894, Jane Bouverie (wife of JASB) who died aged 72 on 22 October 1903, John Augustus Sheil Bouverie (second son of JASB) who died aged 38 on 6 May 1905 and finally Mary Bouverie (second daughter of JASB) who died aged 78 on 20 January 1943.

Visitors to the Church are most welcome contact names are on the outside Church Notice Board.

Chapter 5

DELAPRÉ ABBEY
DURING AND AFTER WORLD WAR TWO
1940 - 48

When Great Britain declares that a state of war exists between it and a third party, as it did in 1939 against Germany, this process brings automatically onto the Statute Book several Acts of Parliament, which give the government of the day wide ranging powers to deal with the situation. A key Act is that of requisitioning Property, and it was under this Statute that the War Office in 1940 requisitioned Delapré Abbey, by formally notifying Mary Bouverie that her property was required for defence purposes by the War Office and she probably received no more than 28 days notice before it was taken over.

Over the years as a Blue Badge Tourist Guide, the question of what happened at the Abbey during the war has often been raised with some quite interesting comments as to the likely activities - these have ranged from training Special Agents for night air drops into France, Holland and Belgium to an Administrative Centre for the former Northamptonshire Regiment barracks at Wootton. The latter is near to the facts.

In 1940 the threat of invasion was real and the bulk of the army had just been rescued from Dunkirk. Churchills government realised that it needed to plan for a large, trained army in order to meet the commitments that quite clearly were going to face Britain in the coming years; the War Office therefore established Infantry Training Centres in nearly all of the Counties in UK. Northamptonshire had its own County Regiment which like many others, had a great history and reputation, its HQ was at Quebec Barracks in Wootton and it was here that men who had been called up for the War, reported for their basic training. The Barracks were not however able to provide what is known as 'Continuation' training - the phase after Basic training, due to a lack of accommodation.

Delapré Abbey was close to the Barracks, had accommodation and in particular extensive land for the more practical aspects of field training needed for the Continuation phase of the overall Infantry training programme. Whilst formal Army records are not available, a report provided by a former 2Lt GLF Ward who returned to Delapré in 1979 to see what was happening there ....the Record Office was then in situ .... provides us with an interesting overview.

An Infantry Training Company occupied the Abbey and he had been a Platoon Commander. It was commanded by a Major (Officer Commanding) who reported to the Commanding Officer, a Lt Colonel in Quebec Barracks. The Major had a 2ic and 3 Platoon Commanders plus a permanent training staff of Sergeants and Junior NCOs.

This team trained the soldiers who numbered about 90 at any one time and were processed through on a Platoon basis (30 men), as one left for their Regiment - another arrived from the Depot. The estate provided a good opportunity for field craft and night manoeuvres and there were many 10 - 15 mile route marches wearing full battle kit in all types of weather. It was also quite common for soldiers who had been wounded in battle to come to Delapré for light duties and recuperation before being sent off again to their Regiment. The Cookhouse had been run by ATS ladies who maintained morale…and he commented on the rivalry and hostility between his soldiers and the Americans based around the town caused by the pretty girls of Northampton!

The Unit's role was run down in the 1945-48 period, as wartime soldiers were demobilised back into civilian life and a smaller, structured training organisation was created to deal with National Service. In 1948 the Unit closed and the Ministry of Works moved in with the County Agricultural Committee.

(see page 25 item 7 for historical evidence)

Chapter 6

THE COUNTY WAR AGRICULTURAL COMMITTEE
1948 - 53

The author is grateful to Joyce Smith for her assistance with this brief historical overview. She worked as a Committee employee initially in the town and then for 5 years at Delapré.

Her first memories of Delapré were however as a 'Young Farmer,' when she met the Farm Manager, a Mr W Ansell, to see the pedigree herd of Red Poll cattle which Mary Bouverie had started.

When the War Department needs for Delapré ceased in 1948, the accommodation was then taken over by the Ministry of Works for its Northamptonshire County War Agricultural Committee. This was a big organisational step forward for the Committee, because it's functions had previously been located in various parts of the town eg: Feed Stuffs in Derngate, Drainage in Bridge Street, Finance and Labour in Lloyds Bank Chambers and the Typing pool in the County Hall. As the UK was in a period of national food rationing, the Committee had the dual responsibility for:

1. Coordinating the agricultural food needs of the County consumer, with the ability of the local farmers to meet the production needs.

2. Providing the farmers with a service for renting farm machinery, providing manpower as required, installing drainage and assisting with Grant applications.

The Ministry had a strategic view of the function, so that a surplus or deficiency in some areas eg milk or vegetables, was balanced by adjacent Counties.

Within the function there were departments for farm machinery, crop advice, cattle advice, milk production and also assistance to farmers on identifying and avoiding agricultural pests and diseases. Joyce remembers that she was the expert in identifying Colorado beetles and kept examples in a matchbox on her desk. When farmers appeared with insects in boxes - she produced the matchbox and in all cases…none were identical!

Inside the Abbey, the Feedstuffs dept occupied the Dining and Withdrawing Rooms on the south side, the Typing Pool was in the Library, and the Telephone Switchboard was by the French Windows leading to the lawn, Joyce was in Finance and the function occupied several rooms on the south facing first floor. The North Wing housed the Advisory Service Officers who were always out and about in the countryside with the farmers. Interestingly the Land Drainage dept/depot was by the main entrance gate opposite the large puddle which still forms today after heavy rain, clearly their budget did not run to 'in house solutions'.... Those staff members who had a car... bearing in mind that this was before the widespread use of anti freeze, had to drain and refill the radiator water before and after use!!

Committee members enjoyed playing sport and were active in the town Table Tennis and Hockey leagues. A local contractor was called in to eliminate the daisy problem on the cricket lawn. He sprayed the lawn to kill off the daisies and to everyone's horror... ..this resulted in an amazing crop of them which only with time gradually disappeared - the cricketers were not amused!

By 1953 the Committee's work had contributed to the phasing out of rationing in UK and they moved from Delapré to take up residence in purpose built offices in Gladstone Road. As they moved out of an increasingly 'tired' building that needed refurbishment, the Estates Department of the Northampton Corporation, now known as the Borough of Northampton, moved in.

Chapter 7

THE NORTHAMPTON CORPORATION ESTATES DEPARTMENT
1953 - 57

Since the purchase of the Abbey by the Corporation in 1946, they had not had a proper opportunity to formally examine exactly what they were getting for their money.....The move therefore of the Estates Department into Delapré Abbey, gave them the ability to establish the actual structural and fabric condition of the property. No doubt the Estates Committee wanted to know exactly what damage had been caused over the recent war years and in particular over the past Century of poor maintenance - enabling them to form a reasonable evaluation of the financial commitment needed for their new asset, in order for the Corporation to plan the Abbey's future. The necessary technical information was obviously given, because in February 1954 the Town Council (renamed from Corporation) voted to demolish the Abbey. The Estates Department however remained there until 1957 when they moved out to premises in the Bedford road.

Chapter 8

THE BATTLE TO SAVE DELAPRÉ FROM DEMOLITION
1954 - 59

Prior to World War 2 the County's Record heritage had been dispersed in various locations for historical reasons but from 1920, the formation of the County Record Society saw a concerted professional effort to persuade the County Council to collect, collate and preserve the County's history. It was however a slow start to a County Council Records function but with the onset of War, the County Council did focus on coordinating and preserving its heritage and the Isham family at Lamport Hall kindly agreed to hold the great majority of the County Records. As the War drew to a close and the 1950's arrived, it was clear that Lamport Hall was no longer suitable as the County Record Office. It was after all a family home, difficult to reach by public transport and space was running out fast.

Dr Joan Wake was the County Record Officer and had been regularly lobbying the County Archives Committee to find a suitable alternative location. When she heard in early 1954 that Northampton Town Council was planning to demolish the Abbey, she realised that this was the ideal location for her Record Office!! and persuaded the County Archives Committee to register their interest in the location with the Town Council. One also has to consider the finances here.......In 1946 Northampton Corporation had paid £56,421 for the Abbey and estate (£1,914,930 at 2012 prices) and yet 8 years later, were demolishing the Abbey - land values obviously being more than the building.

In February 1954 the Town Council voted to give a temporary reprieve to their decision to demolish the Abbey but on 6 April, despite a spirited performance by Alderman Frank Lee that the Council should sympathetically consider a scheme from a 'suitable body' (the County Council) to preserve the Abbey, the Town Council voted by 27 - 16 to demolish it.

This decision did not go down well......On 29 April the Northampton Rural District Council asked the Town Council to 'think again' and also the people of Northampton were beginning to realise what was happening to 'their' Abbey and started a 'Save Delapré Campaign'. On 8 July 1954 Harold McMillan (later to be Tory Prime Minister) but then Minister for Housing and Local Government, met with Borough representatives to discuss the future of Delapré. - no immediate solution was foreseen but demolition was still not cancelled by December 1954.

Throughout 1955 Joan Wake and others lobbied hard for the demolition to be cancelled and an alternative use to be found, the Record Office solution being the preferred option. During the year with Estates Department assistance plus external specialists, a costings project was implemented with the object of assessing the financial commitment necessary to restore Delapré Abbey to an adequate standard for Record Office use.

As 1955 drew to a close, the campaigners suffered a shock on November 16th when the County Council stated that it was withdrawing its objection to the demolition - but the campaigners fought on!! In January 1956 a Public Meeting took place in the Guildhall. This produced two important decisions:

1. Northampton Town Council would grant a six-month 'reprieve' on the demolition decision.

2. Northamptonshire Record Society would start an Appeal for a total of £20,000 (£431,600 at 2012 values) to save the building, enabling it then to be used as the County Record office. The Town Council gave a 6 month limit to the Appeal.

Looking at the 2012 updated value of £431,600 for the total Appeal sum of £20,000 from 1956, one can see the enormity of the task facing the Record Society.....and it was subject to an initial 6 month limit! Cynical hope perhaps that it would not succeed? Due to the illness of Joan Wake, the campaign did not start until 25 February 1956. It had to raise £15000 in four months (£323,700 at 2012 values) and if that was done - the Ministry of Works would then top up with a further £5000 (£107,900 at 2012 values). When one considers that the only media available in 1956 were BBC radio, newspapers and mail shots, TV being limited in coverage and viewers; the motivation of the Appeal Trustees and Record Society Committee has to be admired.

As the Spring of 1956 came and went, the donations were gradually coming in and by early May £3150 had been received. At this stage the Town Council extended the deadline from 30 June 1956 to 28 February 1957 - one year after the start of the campaign. In June an American sent $100 as his ancestors had come from Long Buckby some 316 years previously, July saw a donation of £2000 and by November, £13000 had been reached. On 19 February 1957 the Delapré Trustees (the campaigners title) were able to claim the £5000 grant from the Ministry of Works and thus secure the Abbey and its use as the County Record Office. Restoration work started in the late Spring of 1957 and continued for over 2 years. The workmen found dry rot, wet rot and unsafe areas caused through the ravages of the past 300 plus years and lack of regular maintenance. Stonework was also repaired as required.

Behind the scenes however, Northampton Town Council were busy drawing up a Leasing Contract to effectively let the Abbey at a 'peppercorn' rent plus maintenance to the Northamptonshire County Council. This was duly agreed and in a short ceremony at the Guildhall, responsibility for Delapré was transferred to the County Council from April 1959: ownership however remained with the Town Council.

On the 15 May 1959 the County Record Office was formally opened at Delapré. Over 1100 guests were in attendance on that famous day, Joan Wake's initiative and efforts had paid off some 6 years after she had started. Amongst the many distinguished guests who paid tribute to her in their speeches were Lord Evershed - Master of the Rolls and the Earl of Euston - deputy Chairman of the Society for the Preservation of Ancient Buildings. A well deserved plaque commemorating Joan Wake's success is on the left hand wall of the entrance in the West front of the Abbey. The Northamptonshire Record Society, in view of its enormous contribution to the achievement, was also given Rooms within Delapré.

Joan Wake was born 0n 29 February 1884 and was the second daughter of Sir Hereward Wake the 12th Baronet. She had a distinguished career in which she established the Northamptonshire County Record Society in 1920 and was the author of numerous historical books. She was awarded a CBE in 1960, which followed an earlier OBE. She died on 16 January 1974 some 6 weeks short of her 90th birthday. Without her drive and initiative, Delapré Abbey would not exist today. (see photo 2 on page 24).

Chapter 9

THE COUNTY RECORD OFFICE YEARS
1959 - 1992

The transfer of the County Records from Lamport Hall to Delapré was completed by 1961 and gave the staff the opportunity to assess and evaluate their stock and its condition. Essential to the storage of paper is the elimination of damp and humidity where possible, thus all the fireplaces in Delapré were either boarded or bricked up, a central heating system was also built throughout the house, numerous rooms had an air extraction system fitted which is still there today and in sensitive areas, a fire sprinkler system was also installed.

This work was carried out with thought for the preservation of the Records rather than the building and in doing so, the beautifully decorated ceilings of the Dining Room and Withdrawing Room were subject to damage eg fire alarm sensors, fluorescent lights and air extraction vents. The items are still there but professional opinion is that that they can be removed and the ceiling restored...at a cost. The building was not subject to any preservation order, so the necessary work was done as required. On 9 December 1968 however that all changed.

On that date the Minister for Housing and Local Government signed off a Grade 2 Star Preservation Order under the Town and County Planning Act 1962 Section 32,33,52 and the Civic Amenities Act 1967 which placed Delapré on the list of buildings of Special Architectural or Historic Interest in the County Borough of Northampton. The County Council were therefore constrained in what they could do to the building and Northampton Borough as the 'owners,' were also obliged to ensure that their tenant conformed to the Preservation Order.

Over the years many people visited the County Record Office at Delapré and everyone who had contact with the staff, respected its services. The location also enabled the setting of Delapré Abbey to be appreciated by the many visitors over the years. Northampton Borough maintained the grounds, in particular the enclosed rear Garden was a splendid example of the Gardeners art during the Summer and was much enjoyed by the public. However as the mid 1980's arrived, the problem of storage began once again to rear its head...and the County Council began to look around for an alternative site but the opportunities were poor.

In 1987 the Government reviewed its Civil Defence structure and from that it became clear that Northamptonshire County HQ whilst having adequate facilities, required an upgrade and money would be made available for a suitable site. It was a sensitive subject but the County commenced a review with the Borough in 1988 and the outcome was released to the local press on 18 February 1989 - A Nuclear Protection Bunker would be built in the grounds of Wootton Hall Park and on top of it would be a new County Record Office, the Bunker being a document storage facility in peace time. The first turf was cut on 18 April 1989..........but by Christmas of that year, the potential nuclear threat from the Soviet Communist States had been eliminated in an amazing domino effect of people power establishing their freedom from the state of Communism, following Mr Gorbachov's initiative in the Soviet Union.

The building of the new HQ however continued, no doubt much to the relief of County Council staff and those at Delapré where space was now the big issue......By 1991 the work at Wootton Hall had been completed and the transfer of the County Records from Delapré to their new 'bomb proof ' home began. By the end of 1992 the Records Office had cleared Delapré and once again it was empty.

The Northamptonshire Record Society also moved into the new building at Wootton Hall, where it has an office and excellent collection of specialist County literature in its library.

Chapter 10

THE EMPTY YEARS
1992 - 2000

The County Council were pleased that they now had a proper functional building for their Records Office and initiated several reviews after 1992, to ascertain for what purposes they could use Delapré ... the end result could not be avoided - it was surplus to County requirements, notice should be served on the lease and the Abbey handed back to Northampton Borough Council once their plans for it were clear. The Borough, no doubt mindful of the problems in 1954 -57, were probably not keen to take it back in a hurry without clarification of the maintenance work that had actually been carried out during the lease period - before they assumed responsibility again. A reasonable attitude to take on behalf of the Northampton ratepayers!

During this seven year period, the author was in the role of a Blue Badge Tour Guide who, from the Summer of 1992, took people around the outside of the Abbey and in the Gardens. The building was empty and as each year went by, the frustration of the local people grew at the overall state of it and that it was becoming subject to vandalism. They were all advised to contact their Borough Councillor; whether they did or not ... the Borough successfully initiated a Security Guard system to prevent vandal problems. Eventually however the County and Borough settled their differences and from 2000, Northampton Borough Council assumed full responsibility for the Abbey again.

Chapter 11

Northampton Borough Council Action and Appearance of Community Group - The Friends of Delapré Abbey. (FODA) 2000 - 2003

Following the Millennium celebrations of 2000 and the increasing press reports of Lotto monies being available for various good causes, a number of people in the town began to query why a bid could not be made to restore Delapré Abbey - numerous people asked the author in the Tour Guide role and were advised to contact their local Councillor. That the Borough Council was considering the new 'asset problem' is clear but mindful of the furore in 1954 -55, they mulled over the 'what to do' and 'when' aspect of their new responsibility.

Their decision came in early 2001 when they decided to put the lease out to Tender for business use......It was not what people expected and consequently the local response was one of horror at the thought of losing the estate to private business which would undoubtedly restrict their access to the grounds and Gardens. The people of Far Cotton in particular were vocal in their disagreement and in July 2001, the 'Friends of Delapré Abbey' (Foda) held their inaugural meeting at Delapré. The good local TV and Press coverage of their inaugural meeting resulted in a growing community group that represented a wide cross section of Northampton and County society, The Borough Council realised that the matter was still as sensitive as ever…but they had local elections to worry about on 1 May 2003, so the matter was not a resolution priority. During 2002 plans by a consortium to create a Life Space Project for £40 million were formulated; in summary these foresaw enclosing the land to the East of Delapré in green house style domes similar to the Eden Project in Cornwall and using the Abbey as the gateway to this ecology centre. The architect was Tom Hancock who helped design the London Canary Wharf development.

At the same time a group of people representing the Buddhist group 'Jamyang' put forward plans to use the Abbey as a Buddhist Centre and stated they would put in some £6 million to restore it. Revenue would also be generated from its use for weddings, conferences and Buddhist classes. Jamyang had a track record, as they had successfully converted an old House in South East London for such purposes and had influential support for their bid at London MP and English Heritage level.

The newly elected Conservative Borough Council from 1 May 2003 certainly had their - In Tray - full on Delapré matters when they took up their posts. Having no doubt reviewed the two principal bids, they decided in June to award the lease to Jamyang. … they quickly found out just what the local people thought of that, as demonstrations against their decision took place outside the Guildhall with good coverage from all of the local media and TV. The Friends of Delapré Abbey by this time was making itself felt as an organisation that represented the people and their organisational skills that summer were good.

With the local population clearly against the Jamyang concept.....the Borough Council reread the small print of the lease and found that they could not implement their decision because of the public opposition to it...! After a very stormy debate in the Guildhall on the evening of 31 July 2003, the Borough Council decided that neither Jamyang nor the Life Space project would be considered for the lease, they would instead be creating a Community Trust to manage the Abbey and its Parklands. A classic compromise in many ways and one that certainly did not appeal to Foda of Delapré at the time, who favoured the Life Space project. Quite where the £40 million was to come from for creating it...and who was to fund the operating costs, were uncomfortable questions at the time as the author recalls.

Compromise? Yes - but in hindsight this was a good move by the new Council administration who were perhaps too hasty with their initial decision in the first place. Since those days of Summer 2003 however, a lot of good work has been done by means of a Consultation Group and the Friends of Delapré Abbey were recognised by the Borough as representing the interests of the local people and thus became the only organisation with whom they would discuss matters related to Delapré - a well deserved compliment (See Chapter 15 - Foda).

Chapter 12

THE DELAPRÉ ABBEY CONSULTATION GROUP
2003 - 2008

In the autumn of 2003 the Borough started a Consultation Group for Delapré Abbey with Councillor Michael Hill as Chairman and Councillor Brendan Glynane as his deputy. Other members included Officers from appropriate Borough departments and representatives from: The Friends of Delapré Abbey (including the Chairman), Far Cotton Residents Association, The Pony Club and two Blue Badge Tourist Guides (the author being one of them). The Group met every two months and gradually a way ahead for the Abbey became clear, especially following a Presentation to the Group in November 2004.

The Presentation of November will be seen as a key point for the Abbey's future. The Architectural Heritage Trust's representative (Maria Perks) gave a very good overview of what they do and how they could assist in the various steps necessary to set up a 'Building Preservation Trust' for Delapré Abbey. To include the whole Estate at this initial stage would dilute the aim of conserving and restoring the Abbey and seeking the external funding that is essential to implement that objective.

In the Presentation it was stressed that the first step would be for the Borough to undertake a Conservation study on the Abbey, its Inner Garden and outside Car Park area and - subject to its Report - then create a small group of Trustees for a Delapré Abbey Preservation Trust, in order to facilitate and undertake the task of a Feasibility Study (Options Appraisal). She then outlined the way ahead for the Trustees and the Borough.

The Trustees would have to initiate a Study by independent Consultants who would review the Conservation Study and examine with interested parties, the potential use of the Abbey for Community purposes. Their proposals would be presented to the Trustees, who in turn would recommend to the Borough Council whether or not the Abbey had a use for Community purposes. If not - then another route would have to be found to safeguard its future. If the Trustees recommended Community use with a financially viable implementation plan which the Borough Council found acceptable, then they should grant the Trustees a long lease on Delapré Abbey; with the clear objective of the Preservation Trust assuming full responsibility for implementing the recommended plan for converting, maintaining and developing the Abbey for Community purposes.

At the Consultation Group Meeting in April 2005, Northampton Borough Council announced it had accepted the advice from the Architectural Heritage Trust. It therefore agreed to fund first a Conservation Study and then a plan for a Trust to carry out the Options Appraisal Study for the Abbey. This was much appreciated by all present.

For the remainder of 2005 the Group met at regular intervals and dealt with matters relating to the Conservation Study and items of mutual interest regarding the Abbey. In early 2006 the initial Conservation views were available and the Group took a keen interest in them (see Ch13). In June 2007 the Chairmanship changed after a newly elected Borough Council and Cllr Michael Hill handed over to Cllr Jean Hawkins; the Group's focus however was now on the Trustees and their Options Appraisal process and its progress.

Finally on 14 May 2008 with the publication of the Options for Appraisal Paper; the Chairman - Cllr Jean Hawkins with the support of Foda, decided that the Group had achieved its principal aims with the boxes ticked for: Abbey Conservation Study, formation of a Preservation Trust with its Trustees tasked to produce the Options Appraisal for the Abbey's way ahead. The Chairman thanked all in attendance for their efforts over the past 5 years, which had enabled the Borough Council to initiate work to resolve the aims of the Group, knowing that there was genuine support for the whole project by the local community.

Chapter 13

THE CONSERVATION STUDY
2005 - 2007

The Borough Council appointed the 'Conservation Studio' of Cirencester, a respected Consultancy, with a good track record of services to local government for such projects. During the summer and autumn of 2005 the team of Conservationists and Specialists thoroughly examined the Abbey and on 28 July 05, held the first Public meeting in the library of Delapré to give their initial impressions - which reflected their opinion that the building had an interesting history, had numerous original items of interest eg-ceilings and interior walls of the South Wing and due to Borough maintenance, was dry. Their investigations were ongoing and they would prepare a draft Report for the Borough Council by December 05. This resulted in a final Public meeting in the library at Delapré on 16 March 2006 pending the issue of a final Report in the Spring.

At this meeting chaired by Councillor Michael Hill, the Conservation Studio team led by Director Eddie Booth, gave a slide presentation of their findings and stated in summary, that the Abbey was highly important in a national context due to its history which was supported by evidence. The Chairman then announced that the Borough Council had accepted the principal recommendations of the draft Report and pending the final issue, would be implementing the follow on action for the creation of the Delapré Abbey Preservation Trust. There were several questions from the public, in particular on the subject of bunding part of the estate boundaries - the Conservation team were not able to comment on this aspect as their interest and terms of reference were for the Abbey building and its immediate area - which was reflected in their Report to the Borough Council.

During the remainder of 2006, details were clarified between NBC and the Conservation Studio, which resulted in the adoption of the Conservation Plan by the Council Cabinet on 4 December 2006 and it was published 22 March 2007. It is accessible on the Internet at www.northampton.gov.uk. Type in to the Site Search engine - Delapré Abbey Conservation and the Plan comes up for you to read or download - remember the Copyright aspects!

For those readers who do not have access to the Internet, the principal recommendations are summarised below: (with acknowledgements to NBC)

1. The Borough commissions an Options Appraisal and a Management Plan for Delapré Abbey.
    (Actioned by the Trustees in 2008 See Chapter 14)

2. The following work is required, once a future use for the site has been agreed:

a. The preparation of a detailed scheme for the restoration of the historic interiors

b. The preparation of a scheme to rebuild the Conservatory

c. The preparation of a scheme to reuse the Orangery

d. The provision of Improved visitor facilities Including public toilets and a café. (The HLF bid in 2013 should cover most if not all of these recommendations)

3. A full archeological evaluation of the buildings and the immediate site is undertaken.

4. An assessment of the site's ecological significance is undertaken.

5. The Borough Council ask for the site to be added to English Heritage's Register of Historic Parks and Gardens.

6. The Borough Council designates Delapré Abbey, its Gardens and part of the historic Parkland, as a Conservation Area. (Actioned by NBC 2007 & 2008)

7. The Borough Council considers applying to outside organizations, including the Heritage Lottery Fund and English Heritage, for grant aid. (Actioned by NBC 2010 & 2011)

8. Improvements are made to visitor Interpretations, access and facilities.

The Conservation Plan, which is a 2.5cm/1 inch thick document, is significant because:

a. It details the heritage of the Abbey and thus its significance as a heritage asset to the County and Country.

b. It is the lead document for creating the Options Appraisal assessment which gives the detail on how the Abbey can be brought into effective long term use in a sensitive way.

Chapter 14

THE DELAPRÉ ABBEY PRESERVATION TRUST
2006 - 2012

The Trust was created on 25 April 06 when the six Trustees, including the Chairman - Derek Batten and Company Secretary, met at the Guildhall and received a brief from the Northampton Borough Council Legal department on their responsibilities. The application to create a Limited Company with the title - Delapré Abbey Preservation Trust Ltd - was also completed for processing to Company House and on its return, the Borough Legal Department applied to the Charity Commissioners for and was granted, Charity Status for the Trust.

The formation of the Delapré Abbey Preservation Trust (DAPT) was a milestone in the history of the building and its place in both the town and County's history. It was a creditable outcome for the role of the Delapré Abbey Consultation Group whose proactive attitude since 2003, encouraged the Borough to enable its creation.

The sole aim of the DAPT formed in April 2006 was to achieve a recommendation from an independent Consultancy, on whether or not the Abbey was suitable for Community use and if so - identify potential function usage.

The objectives in the process were:

1. Agree a specification for the Options Appraisal Study.

2. Invite tenders from potential lead Consultants.

3. Interview and appoint the Consultancy.

4. Consider the Consultancy proposals.

5. Recommend appropriate action to Northampton Borough Council for Cabinet approval.

For the balance of 2006 and early 2007 the Trustees settled down to their objectives and working in partnership with the Borough Council and the Architectural Heritage Fund (para 2 of Ch 12) interviewing several appropriate Consultants for the task. In 2007 the Consultancy of Purcell, Miller, Tritton was selected and Niall Phillips as their appointed Consultant, commenced work on the Project. On 2 February 2008 the Consultancy team held their initial meeting for Groups (eg Local History Societies, Residents Associations etc) and interested Individuals (eg Councillors and Conservation Officers etc), followed by a Public meeting on 1 March which was advertised through the local media and consequently well attended.

The 1 March meeting of 2008 gave the public the opportunity to study the Options Appraisal results. The various options were professionally presented by the Consultants on Display Boards in the Saloon area and Abbey Library with the Trustees in attendance for questions etc. This was supplemented by a particularly informative handout document titled 'Delapré Abbey Regeneration Project' which outlined the - 'Emerging Use options and towards a Strategy'. The public were asked to complete Questionnaires based on the document and their impressions from the Day; the overall reaction was very favourable, because they could at last see that something formal was being done to get the process rolling towards restoration.

During the collation of opinions In the Summer of 2008, it began to be clear to the Trustees, Consultants and NBC, that a national financial crisis which would affect all levels and activities in Society - was on the horizon and approaching rapidly. The Trustees however were encouraged to pursue their required objectives and recommended the Consultants Report to NBC. It covered various regeneration matters, a selection of the option proposals are below:

1. The South Range ground floor rooms to be used for Conferences and related functions/events.

2. The South Range upper floor rooms (which are large bedrooms) to be used as Conference/Meeting facilities..

3. The Orangery/Billiard Room to be rebuilt to create a Restaurant facility.

4. The balance of Ground floor rooms to be used for Temporary exhibitions/Abbey Visitor facility.

5. The Home Farm Yard buildings use as either as a location for small business units or Garden/farm produce.

6. Delapré Park has a key relationship with the Abbey and should be subject to a separate appraisal.

7. A timetable for the preparation and submission of a bid to the Heritage Lottery Fund (HLF) for funding the overall projects, subject to Council approval.

In the period late 2008 and until after the NBC elections in May of 2011, the Borough Council and its Officers, continued to evaluate and work on the Delapré Abbey recommendations albeit with a lower priority, in view of the financial planning turmoil which the national financial crisis had created for it. During this difficult period, a separate Appraisal for Delapré Park (6 above) was financed; which confirmed its relationship with the Abbey together with the need to use it as appropriate, when future Abbey developments make it necessary. The outgoing Council Administration In May

2011, left a £600,000 ring fenced budget for Delapré Abbey regeneration, which at the time caused great surprise and pleasure among the local population, judging by the Letter Column of the local Chronicle and Echo newspaper.

The new Administration in May 2011 continued the intent of their predecessors which is that the Abbey should remain in public use - but formal plans needed to be made to enable that to happen and build upon where appropriate, the Consultants Option proposals. They raised the priority, as the NBC financial way ahead was now much clearer and this allowed them to put together a submission to the Heritage Lottery Fund in the Summer of 2011 for Development Grant Funding of Delapré Abbey. To their and the local public's pleasure, the bid received a Round One Pass for £250,600 in September 2011. This sum of money being for the purposes of assisting in the evaluation and preparation of the formal NBC bid, which needs to include and provide: a business plan, undertaking surveys and detailed plans with costs for the *first phase of restoration* - which is the South Wing Dining Room, Withdrawing Room, Saloon and Library and maybe the Billiard Room. This will restore the main rooms back to their former attractive and welcoming state for visitors and provide for their use as an Event / Function space with Weddings for example; this will, critically, provide much needed income each year to reduce the annual maintenance costs.

NBC now had up to 24 months to develop detailed and costed plans for restoring the Abbey, so that they could then submit a Round Two bid for an estimated £3.5 million by the deadline of September 2013; their target submission date is March 2013. The yes/no on the Submission Bid is up to 3 months wait and thus a realistic start date is foreseen by the Preservation Trust as the Spring of 2014. The 6 - 9 month delay between the 'Yes' (hopefully late June 2013) and the start, is due to the need for Architects to produce their plans and tenders to be evaluated for the necessary work that follows. The HLF bid provides for restoration only; plans, which are part of the Bid, must show that they are capable of creating an income from Visitors and Business Functions etc to, ideally, completely offset the annual maintenance costs.

To assist NBC in their task and with due process, the same Consultants (Purcell, Miller, Tritton) who had supported them in 2007/8 were selected - with Niall Philips as their Team Leader. After an agreed Action Plan, the Consultancy team set to work from early 2012 with the object of achieving a draft Business plan for NBC, based on interviews, evaluating skills and costings from appropriate Heritage restoration specialists.; which at the time of writing in October 2012 - is ongoing.

In the August of 2011, NBC advertised for new Trustees, following the retirement of the majority of their predecessors, who with their Chairman Derek Batten, had achieved the objectives set for them by NBC in 2006. In November 2011 the new Trustees met and elected Bill Wright as their Chairman; they then settled in to producing plans to work with the Consultants and NBC towards the HLF submission as their first priority.

The Heritage Open Days of 7, 8, and 9 September 2012 were very well attended, with some 500 hundred plus visitors from in and outside of the County, enjoying the excellent weather and reading the Delapré Abbey Preservation Trust Information Boards set up in the Stables. Trustee Chairman Bill Wright was justifiably pleased with the interest level, which focused mainly on the HLF bid, its potential implementation date and realistic uses for the Abbey by the public.

It is therefore the hope of all concerned in the 2013 HLF bid preparation process - eg: the Delapré Abbey Preservation Trust, Friends of Delapré Abbey and others both in and outside of NBC, plus all those in the Community of Northampton who are supporting Foda events, activities and Tea Room: that by the Spring of 2014, restoration work will have commenced on the South Wing and other parts of the building eg Roofing. This activity bringing at last an end to the further decline and decay of previous Centuries, by conserving and thus recreating a heritage building which on the inside and outside, will give current and future local Community generations and visitors who support it, much pleasure in the facilities and enjoyment from its overall ambience.

In a talk with the author, the Leader of Northampton Borough Council - Councillor David McIntosh, said that he and the Council regard Delapré Abbey and its Heritage Lottery Fund bid, the top priority for them to achieve in 2013. It will add to the value of Northampton's heritage by making the location a very good Community resource, which combined with the 1460 Battlefield's historic significance, creates a major Tourist attraction for the East Midlands and beyond.

Bill Wright the Chairman of the Preservation Trust, said that NBC with the Consultants and the Trust; are currently (Oct 2012) very busy with the detail of the HLF bid and are liaising with them on key aspects of the Project. It is, he said, like a large jigsaw puzzle, where you can see where the piece goes but you are not sure 'when' you can actually place it, as other pieces still have to be agreed before it all begins to form the whole big picture of the way ahead - but we are progressing!!

Chapter 15

THE FRIENDS OF DELAPRÉ ABBEY (FODA)
2001 - 2012

As described in Chapter 11, the Friends of Delapré Abbey came into existence In June 1991, following the Borough Council's action in deciding to open Tenders for a Business Lease at the Abbey - it then discovered how unpopular that move was to the local community (Foda's baptism of action, with Regional media coverage). In the 20 years since those buzzing and heady days of protest, the acronym Foda has become well known to the local Northampton community. Inevitably what started out as a group of enthusiastic local people determined to - save 'their' Abbey sic - had some growing pains on the way to its current status but like all organizations with a similar objective, they mellowed and established a good working relationship with Northampton Borough Council, who is their HQ landlord!!

It is to the credit of locally active members that they give of their free time as Volunteers to work seasonally in the Inner Garden or for example, with Catering Manager Michele Ford in the very popular Abbey Tea Room (open 7 days a week from 1000 -1700hrs except over the Christmas period): thus ensuring that its customers can enjoy refreshments either in peace and quiet by the lawns of the Inner Garden or relax in the spotless Tea Room. Michele is however always grateful for more volunteers .....! (See Chapter 16)

However life does occasionally bring about circumstances which provide much valuable free publicity! This particular instance on 12 February 2010, had the Country smiling at a time when the national financial climate was very gloomy. It was all due to the Borough Council banning Tea drinking in the Gardens because, according to the media - the quietness of the Garden was being disturbed by the sound of people noisily drinking their Tea. Cartoons appeared in the National press with the Sun newspaper being the best, to say that the World heard and read this episode with incredulity on the media and Internet - is an understatement ....NBC Planning Committee of course ran for cover and rescinded their ban 2 days later.......but apparently there were grounds for them to consider some action, as a complaint about music in a Marquee in the Garden had been made. Afterwards the Planning Committee had time to rue their PR handling of the affair ....but it did wonders for attendance figures at the Tea Room and Foda's Office received queries via email from around the World!

Charity status was granted to the Friends of Delapré Abbey Trust in 2006. A measure of its developmental success can be seen by the creation of a new Limited Company - Foda Ltd - from 1 April 2012; following a vote by its members on 2 March 2012, which dissolved the Trust and created a new Limited Company on the advice of the Charity Commissioners. The founding members way back In 2001 never dreamt of such an event but.......time, patience, efforts - and there have been many over the years - bring their achievement rewards eventually.

The Friends have also established Delapré Abbey as a focal point for various local Seasonal events - examples are: Opera In the Library of the Abbey over Winter, CAMRA Beer Festival (now the third largest In UK), Town Carnival start & finish, Heritage Weekend to support the opening of Delapré Abbey, Christmas Craft Fair, Weddings location, enabling the Abbey Outer Garden to be used as an educational location for Nursery children, Talking with Hands - learning courses for Deaf & Dumb Children & Adults, Northants Arts Society's three exhibitions per year, local Garden Club Plant sales and an annual Bardic Picnic. So....It is a broad spectrum of local events and thus can be very busy....look on the Internet Site: www.delapreabbey.org or telephone: 01604 708675 for news.

Barclaycard have an HQ located In Northampton and as part of their employee development, NBC have agreed that they can, with support from Foda, use the Abbey grounds to assess, plan, implement and maintain various Projects which enhance its overall environment. This is a very successful activity to both parties with a Win/Win result at the end of it. Foda certainly appreciate the cheerful way the Barlaycard personnel 'get stuck in' to their tasks eg ground clearance and laying a path; and they in turn clearly enjoy the opportunity to be in the fresh air, creating and contributing to an improved local environment. The Foda Internet Site has fotos of their activities.

There have been four Chairman up to the time of writing (October 2012) they are: Graham Walker (June 1991-July 2010); Adrian Thacker 1 July 2010 - 10 March 2011; Mick Ford from 10 March 2011 - 31 August 2012 and Nicola Hedges 1 September - 21 October 2012.

They were asked the following questions :

1. What was/has been your most satisfying event whilst Chairman?

2. What were your feelings on taking over the Chairmanship?

3. How would you like your contribution to be remembered?

Graham Walker

Graham's interview was interesting as it gave the background to the creation of Foda. He was landlord of the Golden Horse Pub in Far Cotton in 1998 and in the heavy Northampton floods of that year, when the area near the Pub was under water, he found that the crisis produced a tremendous community spirit. He then started, with assistance, the Far Cotton Residents Association in 1998 /99. In 2001 as described in Paragraph One of this Chapter, when NBC decided to put out a Tender for business use of Delapré Abbey, the active local community decided that they must do something to stop it and preserve 'their' Abbey; because the Guided Tourist Walks (by the Author) were making it a place of interest at long last for the Town. Thus they created in June, the 'Friends of Delapré Abbey' to register their objections about tendering to NBC.

In 2001 Graham was surprised and also pleased to be voted Chairman of the fledgling Foda, as he felt that the members had confidence in his ability to do something for the community regarding Delapré Abbey; these expectations however also meant extra work and effort to prevent the whole concept sinking. After some thought about his Chairmanship years, he considered his most satisfying event was in 2003 when NBC handed over the keys of the Stable Block to him, thus enabling Foda to have a formal Office at last for its business. He would like to be remembered as the Chairman who was motivated by his Post and gave much time and effort into getting and keeping Delapré Abbey in the community focus and with NBC; thus assisting in the early years, the slow but overall progress to the now relationship with NBC and the Heritage Lottery Fund support. He handed over the Chairmanship to Adrian Thacker on 1 July 2010 and shortly afterwards 'faded away' to spend more time with his family.

Adrian Thacker
Adrian joined Foda In 2009 and found himself being elected a Trustee in November of that year, followed by election to Chairman from 1 July 2010. On taking over as Chairman, he was aware of the need to get procedures in place to move on the objective of creating a Limited Company; but the staff work with NBC, Solicitors and the Charities Commission all took their time. He made considerable progress towards the objective but stood down in March 2011 to concentrate on his teaching career and family. His most satisfying event was the Christmas Fayre of 2010 which showed how the team spirit of dedicated members could and did produce a very good event which raised a generous sum for the Charity; closely followed by the re- enactment of the Battle of Northampton in July 2010. He would like to be remembered for getting the members to focus on the way ahead to being a Limited Company and the inevitable changes that would follow.

Cllr Mick Ford
Mick said that it had been a busy eighteen months for him as both Chairman and since May 2011 as an NBC Councillor. As Chairman he was particularly pleased with the way that donations to Foda, have now been re-organised, so that they tied into specific projects eg: the 2011 Easter Egg Hunt/Raffle and Summer Choral Evening had financed the Battle of Northampton in 1460 - Battlefield Walk Sign Posts; The Christmas Craft Fair, Children's Art Workshop, Art Workshops x 3, Christmas Choral Evening have all been allocated towards the Greenhouse Nr 2 rebuild; finally - the Opera Evening in January 2012, various donations, including one from St Albans Church, are all going towards the restoration of the Clock Tower and its Bell (completed July 2012) - thus enabling the public and Foda Members to see where and for what their donations are being used.

Mick had previously been Chairman of the Far Cotton Residents Association and thus being elected Foda Chairman had not been too difficult; because he had been a Foda Member for many years and knew the personalities and the external organizations such as Barclaycard, who had and are making a worthy impact to the overall community contribution. He considered that he had regained the confidence of NBC after the very short but administratively busy Chairmanship of his predecessor Adrian Thacker. He would like to be remembered as the Chairman who, building on his predecessors efforts, at long last achieved the making of Foda into a Limited Company from 1 April 2012. Mick stood down from the Post on 31 August 2012 to focus on his Councillor duties but still assists Foda as and when time permits.

Nicola Hedges.

Nicola was elected Chairholder by the Foda Trustees from 1 September 2012 following the departure of her predecessor. She has been a Member of Foda for some 10 years with experience as a Volunteer and Event coordinator and finally as a Trustee for two years prior to her appointment. Something she says, she could never have imagined 10 years ago! Very much aware of the responsibilities the Post has for its Members, she will strive to ensure that Foda objectives are a reflection of its development for the future.

Her predeccessor Mick Ford and NBC, initiated a successful Bid to HLF for funding a Post at Foda to administer Community Events and Public Liaison from early 2013. Nicola says that this will enable Oral History to be a big part of a new Foda project, which will involve talking to the people from History/Heritage and Community organisations; because the Trustees see it as an important fresh opportunity, to engage and share timely, valuable local history and knowledge with them before it is lost. (As the Book goes to Press - Due to unforeseen circumstances, Nicola has stood down from her Post and Trustee role. Her successor is being elected at the next Board meeting.)

Chapter 16

THE VITAL VOLUNTEERS OF DELAPRÉ ABBEY

This Chapter is dedicated to all the Volunteers past and present who have given freely of their time and efforts, especially over the past 11 years since Foda was created in 2001 and the Tea Room from Easter 2007. Their various contributions from Serving, Kitchen duties, basic maintenance (but not in the Abbey itself), Greenhouse restoration, Inner Garden assistance to the NBC Gardener, growing of vegetables for the Kitchen, Function and Event preparation and participation .....the list rolls on!! All of these Volunteers have created the reputation that Delapré Abbey now has within the local Community and it is entirely due to their 'frontline' efforts and that of Foda working with NBC. There are 40 Volunteers working in their various support roles at the time of writing - October 2012.

If you want to be one - Contact Michele Ford on 01604 708675 (1000- 1630hrs)

Volunteers were asked if they wished to be interviewed and comments from those who were available are below: 'Why do you like being a Volunteer at Delapré Abbey' was the question:

Kitchen & Waitress Duties

Gary K. A Volunteer for the past 5 years in the Kitchen, enjoys the Team atmosphere in it and meeting the public. Likes working in heritage surroundings and hopes the HLF bid will happen. He enjoyed an interesting history tour of the outside & inside of the Abbey.

James F. Volunteer since May 2012. Said that he enjoys working in the Kitchen , great Team atmosphere and good rapport, no pressure. His efforts always appreciated by Michele (Manager) and Mark (Chef), Likes meeting the public and finds the atmosphere of the peaceful gardens and lovely old heritage buildings, provide a great place to work in.

Lesley B. Volunteer for the past 5 months as a Waitress for the Tea Room, after retiring. Remembers childhood visits to the Park and surrounding areas of the Abbey and enjoys meeting the public, who are appreciative of what is being done by Foda and NBC to protect the heritage and restore the Abbey. The Inner Garden is for her 'a little bit of magic' just outside the Town!

Marc S. Volunteer for the past 2 weeks as a Waiter/Kitchen Support. Currently in the 6th Form at a local School and wanted to get some Work Experience for when employment ultimately looms after School. He was brought to the Abbey by his grand parents as a boy and thoroughly enjoyed it then - and still does now but is able appreciate it and the development plans much more!

Marion F. Volunteer for the past 3 + years as a Waitress after retirement. Enjoys the surroundings and the historic atmosphere of the whole site and the people who visit it. They are genuinely interested in Abbey developments and local history, which she reads up as a hobby. Likes the Team aspect and meeting the public here at Functions / Events.

Patricia R. Volunteer for 4 + years now, visited one day with her daughter and…..loved the surroundings and heritage - so a Volunteer post was offered as a Waitress, where she likes the Team tempo and atmosphere. She has considerable business experience and assists Michele by being the Wedding / Party Organiser for Foda and has developed her own 'Delapré' brand image for such events which are clearly much appreciated.

Sally S. Volunteer after joining Foda with her husband in 2005 at a Heritage Weekend, as Keith had lived in the immediate area when young and they wanted the Abbey to be preserved and restored. Sally, with a small team of other volunteers, had started the Tea Room at Easter 2007 after discussions with NBC. There had been considerable preparation work needed to the Room/building and to get Chairs/Tables for it but donations and purchases - once the money had been made……had gradually seen it all improve to its current state where she is a Waitress. It is a nice peaceful place to work and meet an appreciative public who like the heritage surroundings.

Maintenance and Décorating Team

Bill M. A Volunteer for the past 5 years and is the Maintenance and Decorating Team Leader. He enjoys making a contribution and gets a lot of satisfaction from it, as it enables the heritage of the whole Site (less the Abbey) to be kept up to a standard compatible with the needs and money available. His major Team project has been the restoration of the Greenhouses over the past 3 years with one more to go…. He enjoys meeting the public in his work and their appreciation of the Team's efforts just makes his day! He would welcome additional Volunteers!

John B. Volunteer for past 18 months with Bill, but a Foda Member for 5 years. Lived as a boy in Far Cotton and had Scouting activities in Delapré Park in the early 1950's. Enjoys working with Bill as a member of the 'Greenhouse Restoration Team' and using his skills on general electrics/maintenance in the Garden/Tea Room area.

Paul C. Volunteer for the past 2 years with Bill, and is a qualified Bricklayer and Stone Layer. After retirement, having been a 'Far Cotton boy' he called into the Northampton Volunteer Centre in St Giles Street and decided that Delapré Abbey was where he wanted to work, with its heritage history and memories. He too enjoys the Team work with Bill and the variety of tasks in particular the work on the Greenhouses

Tony R. A Volunteer for the last 3 years. He met Bill in a Garden Centre and as he enjoyed DIY, found himself in the pleasant heritage surroundings of the Abbey in his Team. He too gets a lot of satisfaction in tackling the various jobs they have to assess and action during the course of the four Seasons.

Gardens

Steve K. Volunteer for over 3 years and wanted to put something back into the heritage and local history aspect of the Community at the Abbey. Allotments are divided up into squares so that people can see by demonstration (good education on growing your own!!) on what you can grow/how/where etc. Flowers are laid on some beds as they act as a natural deterrent to insects - come and learn he said and participate!! Some of the Allotment vegetables find their way into Michele's Kitchen. Thinks the surroundings are really relaxing and the heritage atmosphere is a real bonus for enjoyment.

Right: The Stable Block - Foda's HQ and Tea Rooms.
Below: Michele Ford - Catering Manager

Above: The Tea Rooms.
Right: Bill Marshall - Restoration King of the Victorian Greenhouses.

Chapter 17

THE GHOST STORY

If the Author had received £1 for the number of times the question about Ghosts had been asked…..he and his wife would have retired somewhere near the Mediterranean by now …………!!

The Facts? No one can prove they have actually seen one in Delapré, although numerous 'Psychic Investigators and their equipment' on chilly Halloween evenings over the years…..claim…. 'there is something there!!'

In 2008 the author met a charming and sharp elderly lady at the Abbey with her family. She was a distant relative of Mary Bouverie and during the late 1920's early 30's, had spent Summer holidays with her in the Abbey. She related to him and two other Foda members the following:

One Summer evening she was alone and reading in the Court Room * because Aunt Mary had gone to a Hospital Meeting in Town, where she was the Chairperson. Suddenly the dog started to whine and shiver and she felt a cool 'atmosphere'; as she looked at the door to the corridor, she saw the hooded figure of a Nun dressed in a Blue Habit** walking past………
…she was frightened and when her Aunt returned, told her what had happened. The reply was to the effect - Oh do not worry, she will not harm you!

* The Panelled Room to the left of the main entrance where Victorian Bouveries had held Petty Sessions.
** The Blue Habit was worn by Nuns of the Cluniac Order.

The Abbess List - with kind permission of local Historian - Gary Dorrington.

1145	Azelina	Died	?	1349	Isabel de Thorpe	Resigned	1366
1220	Cecilia de Davantre	Died	1242	1366	Joan Mallory	Died	1394
1242	Agatha de Navesby	Died	1275	1394	Margery Dayrell	Died	1407
1275	Emma Malore	Died	1282	1407	Katherine Wotton	Died	1430
1282	Margery de Wolaston	Died	1296	1430	Margaret Multon	Died	1447
1296	Margery de Brock	Resigned	1319	1447	Avice Sywell	Died	1458
1319	Agnes de Pavely	Died	1327	1458	Gonora Doughton	Died	1481
1327	Margaret de Grey	Died	1333	1481	Joane Doughty	Died	1490
1333	Catherine Knyvet	Died	1349	1490	Joane Chese	Died	1504

1504 Clementia Stocke -
Surrendered to Henry V111 on
16 Dec 1538

Chapter 18

THE INNER AND OUTER GARDENS

These two Gardens are subject to information leaflets, so this is a brief summary.

The Inner Garden is behind the Abbey and access to it is either through the Tea Room or by following the south sidewall of the Abbey and walking towards the Wood, where there is an entrance gate in the Wall. The Garden was the Convent cemetery and also the location for some of the dead from the battle of Northampton. The Nuns probably had their garden for herbs, on what is now the south lawn, supplemented by seasonal fruit and vegetables from the farmers to whom they let Convent land.

The Tates and Bouveries would have improved it over the years, especially the first generation of Tate's after their initial take over in 1546, who had the unpleasant task of removing the Nuns cemetery. Zouch Tate's rebuild circa 1635 located the Kitchen on the north east side adjacent to the new garden. Today it is very peaceful and similar to that of the late Bouverie era, the Borough Gardener lovingly maintains it. Readers are recommended to obtain the Inner Gardens leaflet and then walk around and see the historical 17th C Game Larder, Statues, Peace Pole of 1989, 18thC Tree Training Wall, rebuilt 19C Greenhouses and enjoy the Gardener's efforts, especially in the Summer.

The Outer Garden is also maintained by the Borough and Foda have an NBC Booklet which covers the types of trees. It is defined by a Ha Ha Wall which starts by the gate as you go up onto the South front lawn from the front of the Abbey, it then goes in a circle to the east side and stops by the gate where the path goes out and into the Charter Wood. Within the Garden are interesting trees and several small Copse which enable the bird life to flourish. Hidden away are also the gravestones where the Bouveries buried their favourite dogs and also an early 20thC Water Garden, which was restored in the Autumn of 2011 by means of a Grant from the NBC.

NOTES